SPECIAL FORCES INSIGNIA
British and Commonwealth Units

Unique parachute qualification badge created in 1961 by 21 SAS for members of First Aid Nursing Yeomanry attached to a base signals unit prior to the inception of 63 SAS Signals Squadron; dark blue shield, white parachute with light blue wings; Sw/U.

SPECIAL FORCES INSIGNIA
British and Commonwealth Units
An Illustrated Reference Guide for Collectors

James G. Shortt

ARMS AND ARMOUR PRESS
London New York Sydney

To Lucy and Anthony

First published in Great Britain
in 1988 by Arms and Armour Press, Artillery House,
Artillery Row, London SW1P 1RT.

Distributed in the USA by Sterling Publishing Co. Inc.,
2 Park Avenue, New York, NY 10016.

Distributed in Australia by
Capricorn Link (Australia) Pty. Ltd., P.O. Box 665,
Lane Cove, New South Wales 2066, Australia.

British Library Cataloguing in Publication Data:
Shortt, James G.
Special forces insignia: British and commonwealth
units: an illustrated reference guide for
collectors
1. Great Britain. *Army* – Special Forces –
Insignia – History
I. Title
355.1'4   UC535.G5
ISBN 0-85368-875-3

Edited and designed by DAG Publications Ltd;
typeset by Typesetters (Birmingham) Ltd., camerawork by
M&E Reproductions, North Fambridge, Essex; printed and bound
in Great Britain by Biddles Ltd, Guildford and King's Lynn.

CONTENTS

ABBREVIATIONS
used in this book

In the plate captions

A   Anodized
B   Brass
Bl   Bullion; usually hand-made with gold or silver metallic thread; often with coloured silk highlighting
Bm   Bi-metal
Cw   Machine cotton weave
Cp   Chrome plated
Ec   Cloth embroidered
Ef   Felt embroidered
El   Linen embroidered
Em   Enamelled metal
Ff   Felt stitched to felt
Ml   Metal with clear laminaté
P   Printed, painted or stencilled
Pm   Plastic moulded on to felt
Sb   Stay-brite
Sw   Silk woven
W   Worsted

In the Price Guide:

C   Commonly available
R   Rare
U   Unobtainable
*   Subject to replication or run-ons

INTRODUCTION

In many ways, badges and insignia for special forces and élite units are a contradiction in terms: the role of the special forces is primarily to operate in a covert manner, where insignia would betray them. But in reality the men are soldiers, and insignia do exist. In Britain at least, an unwritten rule among special forces forbids photographs of current operatives in case they could be identified by enemy intelligence and their lives threatened as a consequence. Such pervasive secrecy causes an air of mystique to develop around this area of the military, increasing its attraction to the specialist and leading inevitably to the avid collection of élite unit insignia.

Naturally an informed and specialist knowledge of this insignia is limited among the general public; this volume aims to correct that. The reader should, of course, be aware that collecting anything takes one into the arena of commerce where the profit motive operates, so the buyer should be informed and cautious lest he pay more than would otherwise be necessary. This situation is exacerbated as interest grows in special forces and élite unit insignia – demand increases but supply of 'real material' does not grow to match it. Many imitations and outright inventions exist for purchase by the uninformed: *caveat emptor!* (buyer beware).

The development of élite unit insignia is an interesting historical field in itself and provides numerous anecdotes; for instance, a surviving member of 'L' Detachment told me many years ago how the winged dagger had started life as the flaming sword of Damocles, but thanks to the inaccuracy of a Cairo tailor it became the universal SAS symbol we know today! Many reference works have referred to the SAS badge as 'Excalibur', but this was actually the motif of the first Special Boat Sections. (Universal too is the adoption of the Sykes-Fairbairn fighting knife as the emblem of Commando units – 'the Commando dagger'.) The wings of the SAS are derived from a carving of an ancient Egyptian scarab beetle at what was Shepheard's Hotel, Cairo, while the colours of light and dark blue derive from the fact that early members of 'L' Detachment, SAS, were Oxford and Cambridge Blues. The common link in special forces insignia the world over is the prominence of symbolism and colour, items that reinforce the mystique of the subject.

This book covers the badges, insignia and other emblems connected with the Special Air Service Regiment, Royal Marines Special Boat Squadron, Canadian, Australian, New Zealand and Rhodesian units and SAS-derived units raised in Greece, Belgium, France, Oman and South Africa. The majority of items shown here have been issued for wear or have been obtained from the pertinent military museums. I have, in some cases, had to rely on reputable dealers, and to them I extend my thanks. It is my hope that this small volume will assist ordinary collectors in identifying the genuine articles and attaching a realistic value to them.

BIBLIOGRAPHY

Bragg, R. J. and R. Turner, *Parachute Badges and Insignia of the World.* Blandford Press, Poole, New York, Sydney, 1979.

Davis, Brian L. *British Army Cloth Insignia, 1940 to the Present.* Arms and Armour Press, London, New York, Sydney, 1985.*

Grimshaw, Major L. *Badges and Insignia of the Canadian Airborne Forces.* Private publication.

Rosignoli, Guido, *Army Badges and Insignia of World War Two.* 2 vols. Blandford Press, Poole, New York, Sydney.

— *Army Badges and Insignia since 1945.* Poole, New York, Sydney.

Shortt, James G. *The Paras* (Uniforms Illustrated series number 10) Arms and Armour Press, London, New York, Sydney, 1985.

— *British Special Forces, 1945 to the Present* (Uniforms Illustrated series number 13) Arms and Armour Press, London, New York, Sydney, 1986.

— *The Special Air Service and Royal Marines Special Boat Squadron.* (Men at Arms series number 116) Osprey, London.

Verner, Roger, *International Military Parachutist Insignia.* Private publication.

Westlake, Ray, *Collecting Metal Shoulder Titles.* Frederick Warne, London, 1980.

Wilkinson, F. W. *Badges of the British Army, 1820 to the Present.* 7th edition, Arms and Armour Press, London, New York, Sydney, 1987.*

* Uniform with this book.

PRICE GUIDE

Cap, beret and collar badges

1.	C*	£3
2.	C	£4
3.	C	£4
4.	R	£14
5.	C*	£3
6.	U	–
7.	C*	£9
8.	C*	£7
9.	C	£6
10.	C	£5
11.	C	£1
12.	C*	£7
13.	C	£6
14.	C	£4
15.	C	£3
16.	C	£3
17.	C	£2
18.	C	£3
19.	C	£3
20.	R*	£11
21.	R*	£9
22.	R	£20
23.	R	£25
24.	R	–
25.	R	–
26.	R	–
27.	R	£15
28.	R	–
29.	R	£9
30.	R	£9
31.	C	£2
32.	C	£2
33.	C	£2
34.	R	£18

35.	R	£15
36.	R	£20
37.	R	£15
38.	R*	£10
39.	U*	£25
40.	C	£3
41.	C	£3
42.	C*	£7
43.	C	£3
44.	C	£5
45.	R	£4
46.	R*	£8
47.	R	£5
48.	C	£5
49.	U	–
50.	C	£4
51.	R	£5
52.	C*	£4
53.	C*	£5
54.	U	–
55.	C	–

Arm and shoulder badges and patches

56.	U*	£20
57.	R*	£8
58.	C	£3
59.	R	£4
60.	C	£3
61.	C	£1
62.	C	£3
63.	C	£3
64.	C	£4
65.	C*	£2
66.	U	–
67.	U	£12

68.	C*	£2
69.	R	£4
70.	R	£4
71.	C	£1
72.	R	£3
73.	C	£2
74.	R	£7
75.	R	£4
76.	R*	£5
77.	R	£5
78.	R	£4
79.	R*	£5
80.	R*	£3
81.	R*	£4
82.	R*	£4
83.	R*	£5
84.	R	£4
85.	R	£4
86.	R	£4
87.	R	£4
88.	R	£4
89.	R	£4
90.	R	£4
91.	R	£5
92.	R	£6
93.	R	£8
94.	R	£10
95.	R*	£4
96.	R	£10
97.	R	£6
98.	R*	£5
99.	R*	£3
100.	C	£1
101.	C	£2
102.	C*	£2
103.	R	£15

104.	R	£10	149.	C	£1
105.	R	£7	150.	C	£1
106.	R*	£5	151.	C	£1
107.	C	£4	152.	C	£1
108.	C*	£2	153.	C	£2
109.	C*	£4	154.	C	£1
110.	C*	£2	155.	C	£6
111.	C*	£3	156.	R*	£4
112.	R	£7	157.	C*	£2
113.	R	£7	158.	C*	£2
114.	R	£20	159.	C*	£2
115.	R	£10	160.	C*	£2
116.	R	£7	161.	R*	£5
117.	R	£7	162.	U	£10
118.	C	£3	163.	R	£6
119.	C	£4	164.	R	£10
120.	R	£6	165.	C*	£3
121.	C*	£3	166.	R*	£5
122.	R	£5	167.	R*	£6
123.	U	£9	168.	C*	£2
124.	R	£8	169.	R*	£8
125.	R	£10	170.	R*	£13
126.	R	£2	171.	R	£6
127.	R	£6	172.	C	£2
128.	R	£8	173.	U	–

Rank insignia

192.	C	£3
193.	R	£6
194.	C	–
195.	C	–
196.	R	£15
197.	R	£4
198.	R	£8
199.	C	–
200.	R*	£6
201.	C	£3
202.	R*	£5
203.	R	£10
204.	R*	£6
205.	R*	£7
206.	R	£8
207.	C	£7

Rank insignia

208.	C	£5
209.	R	£3
210.	R	£4
211. 212.	R	£5
213.	R	£7
214.	R	£9
215.	R	£11

Epaulette slides

216.	R	£7
217.	R	£5
218.	R	£9
219.	C	£4
220.	C	£4
221.	C	£4
222.	C	£4
223.	C	£4
224.	C	£4
225.	C	£4
226.	C	£4
227.	C	–
228.	R	£5
229.	C	£4
230.	C	£4
231.	C	£4
232.	C	£4

129.	C	£3
130.	R	£6
131.	C	£2
132.	R	£4
133.	C	£6
134.	C	£6
135.	C	£6
136.	C	£6
137.	C	£8
138.	R	£10
139.	C	£3
140.	C	£3
141.	C	£3
142.	C	£3
143.	C	£3
144.	C	£1
145.	C	£1
146.	C	£1
147.	C	£3
148.	C	£1

Parachute wings

174.	C	£3
175.	R	£6
176.	C	£3
177.	C	£2
178.	R	£4
179.	C	£1
180.	R*	£6
181.	R*	£10
182.	R*	£7
183.	R*	£7
184.	R*	£5
185.	C	£2
186.	C	£1
187.	C	£2
188.	C	£1
189.	C	£2
190.	C	£2
191.	C	£4

233.	C	£4	**Regiment and unit**			276.	R	–
234.	C	£4	**association insignia**			277.	R	–
235.	C	£4	254.	R	£3	278.	R	–
236.	C	£4	255.	R	£3	279.	C	–
237.	C	£3	256.	R	£3	280.	C	–
238.	C*	£5	257.	R	£3	281.	C	–
239.	C*	£6	258.	R	£3	282.	C	–
240.	C*	£7	259.	R	£3	283.	R	–
			260.	R	£3	284.	R	–
Stable belts			261.	R	£3	285.	C	–
and buckles			262.	R	£3	286.	C	–
241.	R	£12	263.	R	£3			
242.	C	£10	264.	R	£3	**Regiment, unit and**		
243.	C	£11	265.	R	£3	**association plaques**		
244.	C	£10	266.	R	£3	287.	R	£3
245.	C	£10	267.	R	£3	288.	R	£3
246.	C	£4	268.	R	£3	289.	R	£3
247.	R	£25	269.	R	£3	290.	R	£3
248.	R	£8	270.	R	£3	291.	R	£3
249.	C*	£3	271.	R	£3	292.	R	£3
			272.	R	£3	293.	R	£3
Unofficial unit						294.	R	£3
emblems			**Regiment, unit and**			295.	R	£3
250.	R	£2	**association ties**			296.	R	£3
251.	R	£4	273.	R	–	297.	R	£3
252.	R	£4	274.	R	–	298.	R	£3
253.	R*	£2	275.	R	–	299.	R	£3

ACKNOWLEDGEMENTS

I should like to express my gratitude to the following establishments, organizations and individuals who have provided assistance in obtaining the material to produce this work: Major M. J. Rees, MM, Captain D. Blackwood, Lieutenant E. M. Roles, Flying Officer D. M. MacKay, BA, RAF, Warrant Officer G. Burroughs, RE, Warrant Officer D. Wassall, RM, Sergeant D. Major-Baron, Sergeant P. Williams, RM, Sergeant N. Devenish, RM, Marine S. Bell, RM, Senior Aircraftsman N. Furlong, RAF; David Penn and Ray Allan of the Imperial War Museum, London; David Ball (1 Commando); Ray Rodley, Rosemary Eldridge, James Gee and Andrew Butler. Items depicted were generously loaned by: The Imperial War Museum; SAS Regimental Association; 2 Para Sqn, RAF Regt; 148 (Meiktila) Cdo F O Bty, RA, UFI, RM Poole; HQ Trng Reserve and Special Forces, RM; Cash Clothing CTC, RM; SPRO Flag Officer Plymouth; The Parachute Regiment Association; CE Commando, Regt Para-Cdo, Belgium; Airborne Forces Museum; Special Forces Club; Victoria Badge Company; Toye, Kenning & Spencer.

CAP, BERET AND COLLAR BADGES

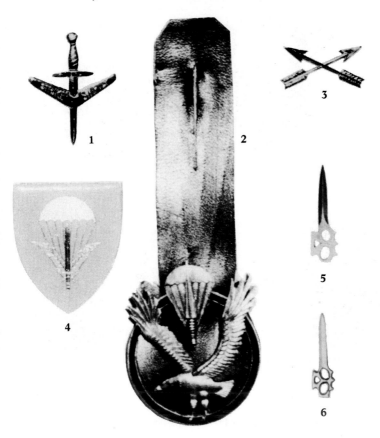

1. Australian 1 Commando Regiment cap badge; anodized white dagger and yellow boomerang; A/R.

2. Belgian 1 Cie Equipes Spéciales de Reconnaissance (1BE) pocket fob, current; grey eagle, parachute and dagger with black circle on leather fob; M/R. (This badge is also the emblem of the International LRRP School in Germany, which is staffed by the British SAS, Belgian ESR and German FernspähtKompani.)

3. 1st Canadian Special Service Battalion collar badge, US-pattern World War Two; yellow metal; B/R.

4. Ciskei Special Forces (ex-Rhodesian Special Forces); white parachute, light blue wings, silver detail and sword, black pommel, grey field; Ml/R.

5. 50–52 Commando, Middle East, first version cap badge, World War Two; yellow metal; M/U.

6. 50–52 Commando, Middle East, (later 2 SAS) second version cap badge, World War Two; brass; B/R.

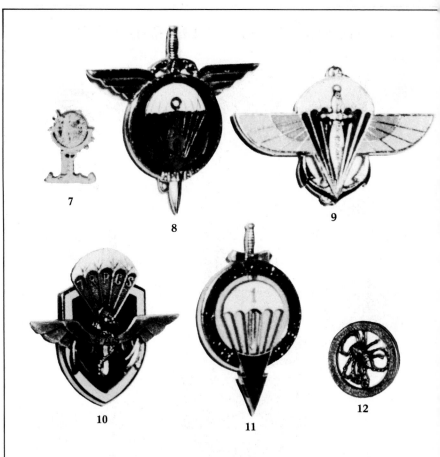

7

8

9

10

11

12

7. 1st Demolition Squadron (Popski's Private Army) cap badge, World War Two; white metal theodolite; M/R.

8. French 6 Régiment Parachutiste Infanterie de Marine (also 6 Battalion Colonial de Commando Parachutistes, 1948); gold sword and wings with SAS on quillon, black field, white parachute red anchor and blue numeral, gold circlet and lettering; EM/C.

9. French 2 Régiment Parachutiste Infanterie de Marine, 1955; gold anchor, light blue and dark blue SAS parachutist wings, white parachute on red field, gold detail, silver sword with motto *Qui ose gagne* (Who dares wins); EM/C.

10. French 7 Régiment Parachutiste Infanterie de Marine (also 7 Battalion Colonial de Commandos Parachutistes BCCP and 7 Regiment Parachutistes Colonials); grey parachute and wings with 7 RPIMa and SAS, gold anchor on maroon shield with light blue border, highlighted in silver; EM/C.

11. French 1 Régiment Parachutiste Infanterie de Marine (also previously 1 Demi-Brigade SAS [Indochina]), current; gold sword, white parachute, gold number, silver circlet, blue field, red arrowhead, black lettering; Em/C.

12. Long Range Desert Group cap badge, World War Two; brass scorpion enclosed in circlet; B/C.

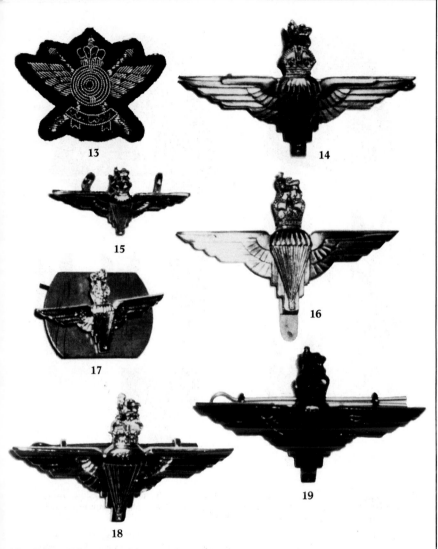

13. Oman, Sultan's Special Forces beret badge, current; gold bullion embroidered on felt; Bl/R.

14. Parachute Regiment cap badge (King's crown), World War Two; white metal; M/C.

15. Parachute Regiment collar badge (King's crown); white metal; M/C.

16. Parachute Regiment cap badge (Queen's crown); white metal; M/C.

17. Parachute Regiment cap badge (Queen's crown), current; white anodized metal, brass backing plate and split pin; A/C.

18. Parachute Regiment cap badge, current; white metal anodized; A/C.

19. Parachute Regiment (Tactical), current; black anodized metal; A/C.

20. Raiding Support Regiment first issue beret badge, World War Two; light blue winged gauntlet, white hand, tower and lettering; black motto on white scroll; trimming in red on dark blue field; Ef/R.

21. Raiding Support Regiment, second issue beret badge, World War Two; light blue winged guantlet, white hand, tower and lettering; black motto on white scroll; trimming in red on khaki field; Ef/R.

22. Rhodesian SAS cap badge; anodized yellow metal wing and scroll, white metal sword; A/R.

23. Rhodesian Grey's Scouts cap badge; white metal; M/C.

24, Rhodesian SAS first, second and third issue collar badges; anodized yellow metal
25, wings and scroll, white metal sword; A/R.
26.

27. Rhodesian SAS cap badge (made by Reuteler MFG, Salisbury); bronze; M/R.

28. Rhodesian SAS-attached 'Psyops' unit cap badge; chromed metal; Cm/R.

16

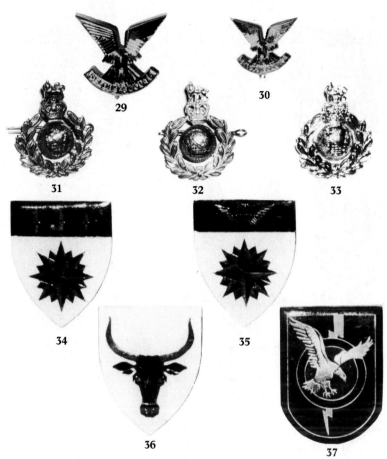

29. Rhodesian Selous Scouts cap badge; white metal; M/C.

30. Rhodesian Selous Scouts collar badge; white metal; M/C.

31. Royal Marines cap badge (King's crown); brass; B/C.

32. Royal Marines cap badge (Queen's crown); brass; B/C.

33. Royal Marines cap badge, current; anodized metal; A/C.

34. South African 1st Recce; 3 gold Commando daggers on black field, gold compass mark on white; Ml/R.

35. South African 5th Recce; gold Selous Scouts parachute wings on black field, gold compass mark on white field, black detail; Ml/R.

36. South African 52 Counter-Insurgency Battalion; buffalo head black, gold horns and detail on white field; Ml/R.

37. South African Harbour and Railway Police Special Task Force; gold eagle, white lightning bolt, dark blue field, green circlet and border, red bull's-eye beneath clear plastic laminate; Ml/R.

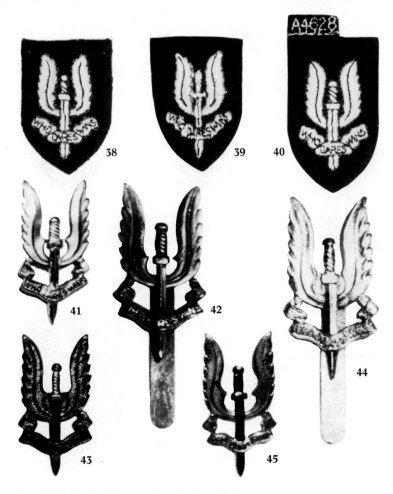

38. Special Air Service Regiment beret badge; Ef/R.

39. Special Air Service Regiment beret badge, Cairo-tailored version, World War Two; S/U.

40. Special Air Service Regiment beret badge, current; Ef/C.

41. Special Air Service Regiment collar badge, World War Two; gold wings and scroll, silver sword; Bm/U.

42. Special Air Service Regiment cap badge, post World War Two; brass; B/C.

43. Special Air Service Regiment first version collar badge, post World War Two; brass; B/R.

44. Special Air Service Regiment officer's cap badge; yellow metal wings and scroll with white metal sword; Bm/R.

45. Special Air Service Regiment officer's collar badge; bimetal, yellow metal wings and scroll with white metal sword; Bm/R.

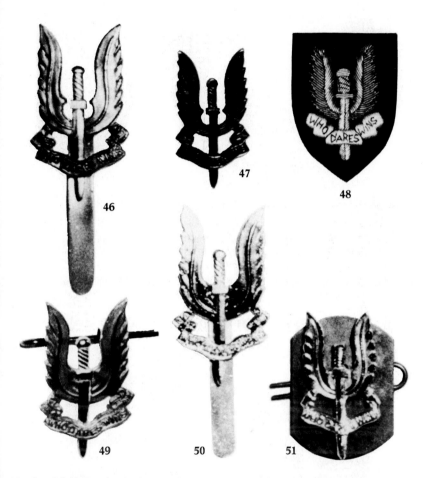

46. Special Air Service Regiment other ranks' cap badge; brass wings and scroll with white metal sword; Bm/C.

47. Special Air Service Regiment second version collar badge; brass; B/R.

48. Special Air Service Regiment officer's beret badge, current; gold bullion wings on silver-wire sword, blue scroll detail and motto in black, highlighting in red on dark blue field; Bl/C.

49. Special Air Service Regiment officer's collar badge, current; gold wings and scroll with silver sword; Bm/R.

50. Special Air Service Regiment other ranks' cap badge, current; anodized bimetal; A/C.

51. Special Air Service other ranks' collar badge; anodized bimetal; A/C.

Metal collar badges are worn by personnel of SAS units; the only metal cap badge worn by SAS was by 21 SAS in 1953. The Australian SAS Regiment, however, does wear a metal cap badge in conjunction with a dark blue cloth shield.

19

52. Artists' Rifles (28th Battalion, The London Regiment); brass; B/R.

53. 21 Special Air Service Regiment (Artists' Rifles) cap badge; white metal; M/R.

54. Special Boat Section cap badge, World War Two; enamelled metal, red lettering, white sword, light blue and white sea, pink arm with white edging on dark blue field; Em/U.

55. Transkei Special Forces cap badge; white metal wings, yellow metal scroll and leopard head; Bm/R.

ARM AND SHOULDER BADGES AND PATCHES

56. First Allied Airborne Army (including SAS Brigade), first issue, World War Two; white numeral, yellow wings on blue field, yellow lettering on black field, white swords crossed on red strip; Ef/U.

57. First Allied Airborne Army, second issue, World War Two; white numeral, yellow wings on blue field, yellow lettering on black field, white swords crossed on red strip; Ef/R.

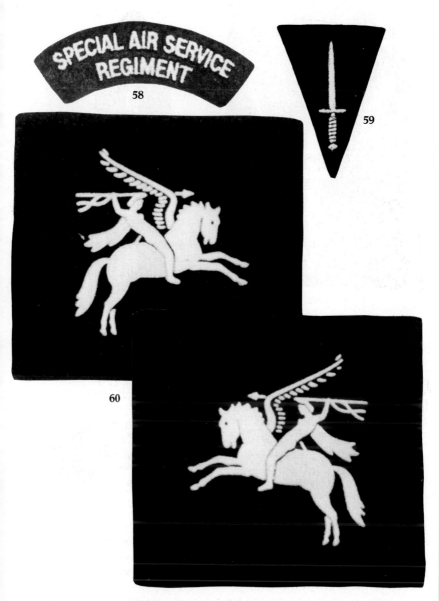

58. Australian Special Air Service Regiment; white lettering on red field; Ef/C.

59. Belgian 2 Commando Battalion; white detail on black field, black overlocking; Ef/C.

60. Belgian 1 Bataljon Parachutisen, current; light blue plastic moulding on maroon felt; C.

61. Belgian Regiment Para-Commando (including 1 Para Battalion) beret, current; white plastic moulded on to black felt; C.

62. 1st Canadian Special Service Battalion (1 SSF 'Devil's Brigade'), World War Two; red arrowhead overlocked in red and white lettering; Ec/R.

63. Canadian Special Service Force best dress insignia (current); gold wings and scroll with black lettering, white sword and detail on very dark green cloth; Ef/C.

64. Canadian Special Force subdued insignia, current; light green wings and scroll on dark green field and lettering, white sword overlocked in olive green; Ec/C.

65. Chindit, Fourteenth Army, World War Two; white border and lettering on black field; Ef/C.

66

67

68

66. Combined Operations pair of arm badges, World War Two; red detail on blue field; P/U.

67. Combined Operations pair of arm badges, World War Two; red detail on dark blue field; Ef/C.

68. Commando, World War Two; red lettering on black field; Ef/C.

23

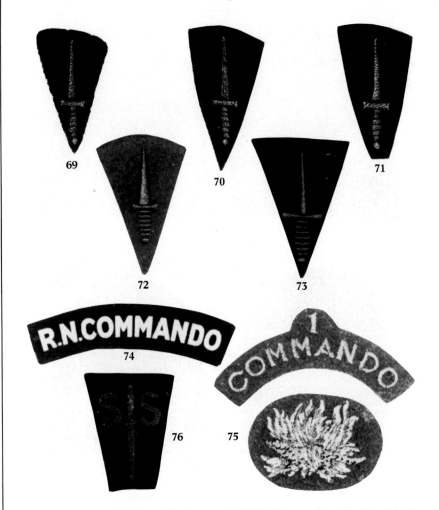

69. Army Commando badge, early pattern, World War Two; red detail on black field; Ef/R.

70. Army Commando badge, 1943, red detail on black field; Ef/R.

71. Commando badge, 1944; red detail on dark blue field; Ef/R.

72. Army Commando badge, late pattern World War Two; yellow on khaki field; Ef/C.

73. Army Commando Badge, late pattern World War Two; red detail on dark blue field; Ef/C.

74. Royal Navy Commando, World War Two; white lettering on blue field; P/R.

75. 1 Commando shoulder flash with unit badge, World War Two; green number and lettering on khaki with green salamander in red and yellow flames; Ef/R.

76. 2 Commando, World War Two; silver detail on black field; Bl/R.

24

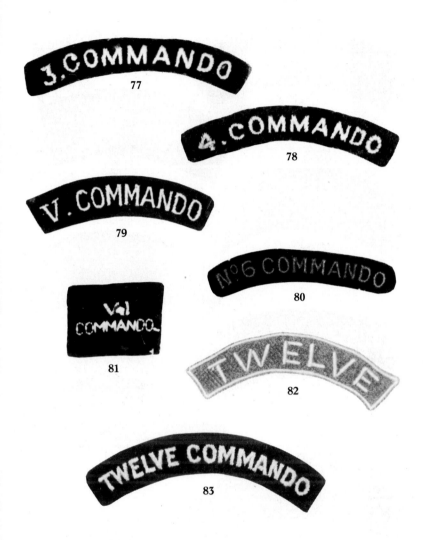

77. 3 Commando, World War Two; white detail on black field; Ef/R.
78. 4 Commando, World War Two; red number with white lettering on black field; Ef/R.
79. 5 Commando, World War Two; white lettering on black field; Ef/R.
80. 6 Commando, World War Two; red lettering on black field; Ef/R.
81. 6 Commando, World War Two; white detail on black field; Ef/R.
82. 12 Commando, World War Two; yellow edging and lettering on blue field; Ef/R.
83. 12 Commando, World War Two; yellow lettering on green field; Ef/R.

84. Rare printed badges from World War Two; all are in red lettering on dark blue field;
94. 94 represents Commando Depot.

92

93

94

95

96

97

98

95. Commando Depot, World War Two; white skull within white 'D' on a khaki field; Ef/R.

96. Commando Signals, World War Two; red script on blue field; P/R.

97. 2 Medical Commando, World War Two; white lettering on blue field; Ef/R.

98. Royal Marine Commando, current; red lettering on dark blue; Ef/C.

99
100
101
102
103
104
105
106

99. Royal Navy special quality Commando badge, current; red silk thread on dark blue; Ef/R.

100. Royal Navy Commando flash, current; white lettering on black field; Ef/R.

101. Army Commando badge, current; red detail on dark blue field; Ef/C.

102. 1st Demolition Squadron (Popski's Private Army), World War Two; white lettering on black field; Ef/C.

103. Force 135, Channel Island Liberation Force, World War Two; the arms of Jersey and Guernsey, three gold lions on red field; Sw/R.

104. Free French Commando, World War Two; red lettering on dark blue field; P/R.

105. 46 Independent Beach Group, RN, World War Two; red and blue detail on white field; P/R.

106. US paratrooper insignia used by SF Jedburgh Teams, World War Two; white parachute within white circle on light blue field (infantry); Ec/R.

107

108

109

110

111

112

107. Joint Services Amphibious Warfare School and 148 (Meiktila) Commando Battery, Royal Artillery, current; red detail on dark blue field; Ef/C.

108. Long Range Desert Group, World War Two; red lettering on black background; Ef/C.

109. New Zealand 1st Special Air Service Squadron; light blue lettering on maroon; Ef/C.

110. Parachute Regiment, World War Two; light blue lettering on maroon field; Ef/C.

111. Parachute Regiment, World War Two; dark blue lettering on light blue field; Ef/C.

112. Rhodesian Army, white lion and pick, green field, red division and overlock; Ec/C.

113. Rhodesian Army Special Forces; white field, black scorpion, black overlock; Ec/R.

114. Rhodesian 1st Brigade; red field, black elephant head, white surround, black overlock; Ec/R.

115. Rhodesian 2nd Brigade; white rhino head, green field, white overlock; Ec/R.

116. Rhodesian 3rd Brigade; brown field, white detail and overlock, black bison head; Ec/R.

117. Rhodesian 4th Brigade; orange/black/white lion head, blue field, black overlock; Ec/R.

118. Royal Air Force Regiment, current; light blue on dark blue field; Ef/C.

119. 2 Field (Parachute) Squadron RAF Regiment subdued pattern, current; black detail on olive-green field, overlocked in olive green; Fc/R.

120. Beach Group, Royal Marines, World War Two; red and blue details on white field; P/R.

121. 101 Troop (SBS) Dover arm badge, World War Two; white swordfish, red numerals on dark blue field; Ef/U.

122. Special Boat Section first pattern, World War Two; red lettering on blue field; P/U.

123. Special Boat Squadron second pattern, World War Two; red lettering on black field; Ef/C.

124. Royal Marines Swimmer-Canoeist Class 3 [SBS], special quality; bullion detail on dark blue, Bl/R.

125. Royal Marines Swimmer-Canoeist Class 2 [SBS], special quality; bullion detail on dark blue field; Bl/R.

126. Royal Marines Swimmer-Canoeist Class 1 [SBS], special quality; bullion detail on dark blue field; Bl/R.

127

128

129

130

127. Royal Marines Mountain Leader Class 2 (Mountain and Arctic Warfare Cadre), special quality; bullion detail on dark blue field; Bl/R.

128. Royal Marines Mountain Leader Class 1 (Mountain and Arctic Warfare Cadre), special quality; bullion detail on dark blue; Bl/R.

129. Royal Marines sniper qualification badge, CTC Lympstone; bullion detail on dark blue field; Bl/C.

130. Royal Navy Submarine Parachute Assistance Group parachute qualification; red silk on dark blue field; Ef/R.

Up to 1987 Royal Marines wore their special quality badges on their Lovat dress; thus all such badges were on a bottle green field. Since that date, these badges are worn on blues, and the badges therefore have a dark blue background, as in the Royal Navy equivalents.

131

132

133

131. Royal Navy Submarine Parachute Assistance Group first issue parachute qualification badge; gold wire embroidered on dark blue field; Bl/C.

132. Royal Navy Submarine Parachute Assistance Group second issue parachute qualification badge; gold wire embroidered on dark blue field; Bl/R.

133. Royal Navy diver's badge, current issue; in gold wire with scarlet detail on dark blue; pair of badges; C.

134

135

136

137

134–Royal Navy diver's badges, current issue; all in gold wire with scarlet detail on dark
37. blue; C. **134** Ship's diver; **135** Clearance Diver 3rd Class; **136** Clearance Diver 2nd
Class; **137** Clearance Diver 1st Class.

138–Royal Navy diver's badges; all in red silk on dark blue cloth; C. **138** set of Clearance
43. Diver 1st Class badges (King's crown); R; **139** set of Clearance Diver 1st Class
(Queen's crown); **140** Ship's Diver; **141** Clearance Diver 3rd Class.

34

138

139

140

141

35

142

143

144

145

146

147

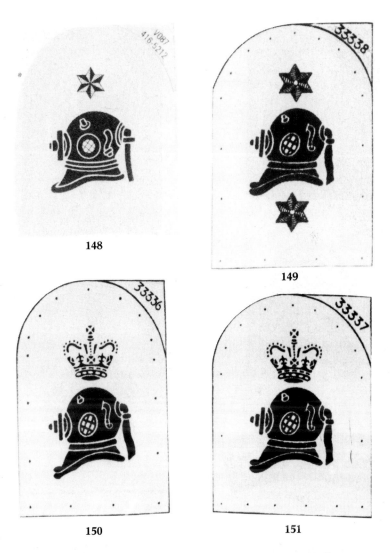

148

149

150

151

142–Royal Navy diver's badges; in red silk on dark blue cloth; C. **142** Clearance
43. Diver 2nd Class; **143** Clearance Diver 1st Class.

144–Royal Navy diver's badges, current; all are embroidered dark blue on white cotton
46. drill; C. **144** Ship's Diver; **145** Clearance Diver 3rd Class; **146** Clearance Diver 2nd
Class.

147–Royal Navy diver's badges; all are printed in dark blue on white cotton drill. **147**
51. Ship's Diver; **148** Clearance Diver 3rd Class; **149** Clearance Diver 2nd Class; **150**
Clearance Diver 1st Class (first version); **151** Clearance Diver 1st Class (second
version).

152. Royal Engineers Advanced Diver; yellow diver's helmet on khaki field; Ef/C.

153. Royal Engineers Compressed Air Diver (Shallow Water); yellow diver's helmet and lettering on khaki field; Ef/C.

154. Royal Engineers Diving Supervisor; yellow diver's helmet on khaki field; Ef/C.

155. South African 5 Recce Patch (ex-Selous Scouts); white field and dagger blade, handle brown, brown/red/yellow snake head, yellow scroll, black overlock and lettering, royal blue wings; Ec/R.

156. 'Layforce' Detachment, Special Air Service, World War Two; white cyphers on maroon field; Ef/R.

157. 1, 2, 3 and 4 SAS, World War Two; light blue lettering on maroon field; Ef/C.
60.

161. Special Air Service Brigade, World War Two; white lettering on maroon field; Ef/R.

162. 21 SAS (Artists' Rifles), 1947; white sword, light blue wings and scroll, black
lettering and detail, red highlighting on dark blue field; Ef/C.

163. Special Air Service Regiment (Artists' Rifles), 1947; light blue lettering on maroon
field; Ef/R.

164

165

166

167

168

169

170

164. Malayan Scouts (SAS Regiment), 1950; light blue lettering on maroon field; Ef/C.

165. Malayan Scouts, 1950; white Malayan kris, white scroll and SAS cyphers with white border on black field with black letters; royal blue wings edged in white; Ef/C.

166. 21 Special Air Service (Artists' Rifles), 1953; light blue lettering on maroon field; Ef/R.

167. 21 SAS (Artists' Rifles), 1954; grey detail on black field, lettering in black; Ef/U.

168. Special Air Service Regiment, light blue lettering on maroon field; Ef/C.

169. 4 Special Service Brigade, 1943; white letters, red roman numerals on black field; Ef/R.

170. Signals, Special Service Brigade Headquarters, World War Two; white detail and cyphers on blue field; Ef/R.

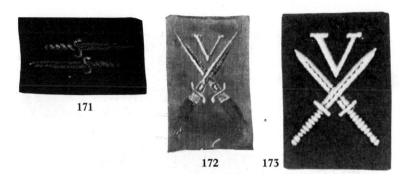

171. Special Service Brigade Headquarters, World War Two; silver knives with red 'SS' quillons on black field; Bl/R.

172. 'V' Force (Far East) first issue badge, World War Two; yellow detail on green field; S/U.

173. 'V' Force (Far East) second issue badge, World War Two; yellow detail on khaki; Ef/C.

PARACHUTE WINGS

174. Australian 1 Commando Regiment, Summer Dress; white detail on beige; Ec/C.

175. Australian Special Air Service Regiment, Summer Dress, first pattern; white parachute, dark blue upper wings, light blue lower wings on beige; Ec/C.

176. Australian Special Air Service Regiment Summer Dress, second pattern, current; white parachute, dark blue upper wings, light blue lower wings on beige; Ec/C.

177. Belgian Regiment Para-Commando, current; white parachute, light blue wings, khaki field and trim; Sw/C.

41

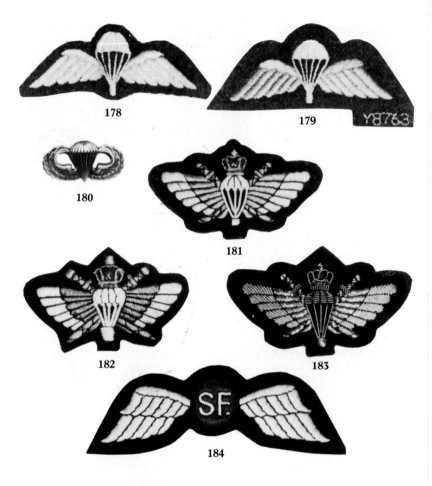

178. Parachute wings, World War Two; white parachute, blue wings on khaki field; Ef/R.

179. British Army parachute wings, current; white parachute, light blue wings on khaki field; Ef/C.

180. 1st Canadian Special Service Battalion, US-pattern; white metal; M/C.

181. Oman, Sultan's Special Forces, first version; yellow and red swords and crown superimposed on SAS parachute wings; Ef/R.

182. Oman, Sultan's Special Forces, second version, current; yellow and red swords and crown superimposed on SAS parachute wings; Ef/R.

183. Oman, Sultan's Special Forces Dress Parachute Wings, current; bullion gold parachute, swords & crown, red embroidery and silver wings; Bl/R.

184. OSS parachute wings (Jedburgh Teams), World War Two; white wings, white lettering on red field, all on blue field; Ef/C.

42

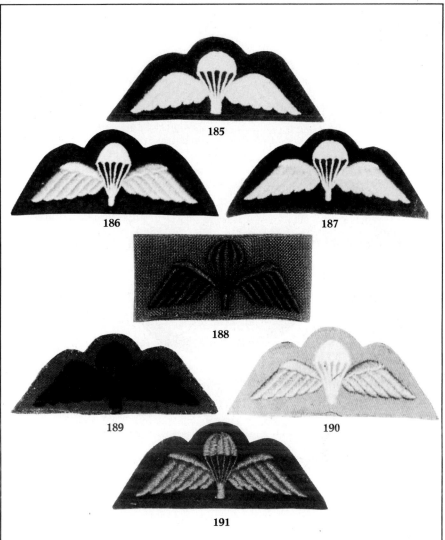

185. Royal Air Force, current; white parachute, light blue wings on dark blue field; Ef/C.

186. Royal Air Force, current; white parachute, light blue wings on dark blue field; Ef/C.

187. Royal Air Force, shirt, current; white parachute, light blue wings on dark blue field; Ef/C.

188. Royal Air Force, subdued pattern; black detail on nylon strap; E/C.

189. British Army, subdued pattern, current; black parachute and wings on olive green field; Ec/C.

190. Royal Marines, tropical; white parachute, light blue wings on sand cotton drill; Ec/C.

191. Royal Navy and Royal Marines, red silk on dark blue field; Ef/C.

192. Royal Navy and Royal Marines (also used on Army No. 1 Dress); silver wire parachute, bullion wire wings on dark blue field; Bl/C.

193. Rhodesian Army (1 RLI Commando, etc.) white parachute, light blue wings on dark green field; Ef/C.

194. Rhodesian SAS, first issue; on olive drab field; Ec/R.

195. Rhodesian SAS, second issue; Ef/C.

196. Rhodesian SAS, Dress; white parachute, dark blue upper wings, light blue lower wings on dark green field; Ef/C.

197. Rhodesian Selous Scouts; bronze; M/C.

198. South Africa; white parachute, silver wings, light blue field; Em/C.

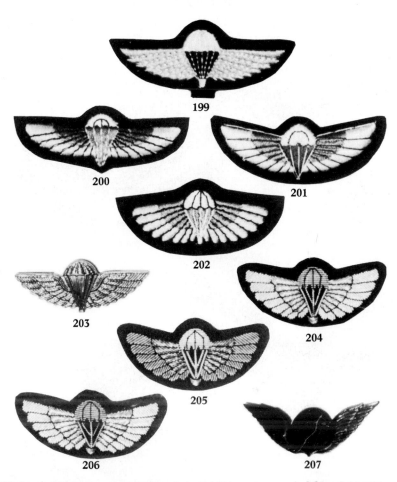

199. South African Recce; white parachute, light blue wings on dark blue field; Ef/R.

200– Special Air Service Regiment; white parachute, medium royal-blue upper wing,
2.   light blue lower wing on dark blue field. **200** World War Two; Ef/R; **201** current
     issue; Ef/C; **202** 23 SAS, current issue; Ef/R.

203. Special Air Service Regiment No. 6 Dress (tropical), post World War Two; brass
with two eyes and split-pin back; B/C.

204. Special Air Service, No. 1 Dress, current; gold bullion parachute, silver wire wings,
black detail on dark blue field; B/R.

205. Special Air Service Officer's No. 1 Dress, current; silver wire parachute with gold
bullion wings, black detail on dark blue field; B/R.

206. Special Air Service Mess Kit, current; gold bullion parachute, silver wire wings,
black detail on red field; Ef/R.

207. Transkei Special Forces (ex-Selous Scouts); bronze; M/R.

45

RANK INSIGNIA

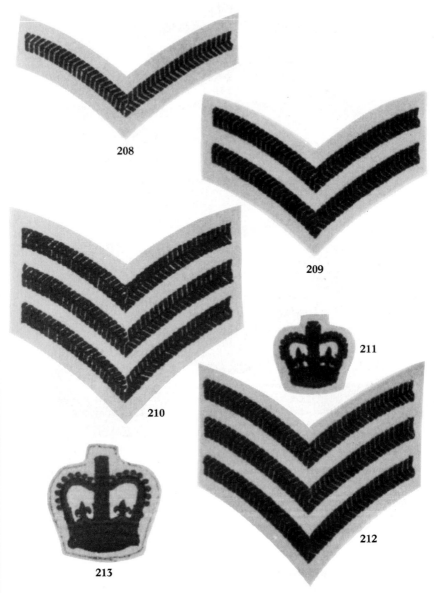

208–Special Air Service Regiment as worn on No. 2 Dress; colours for 22 SAS and 23
14. SAS are dark blue detail on Pompadour blue field; colours for 21 SAS are black
detail on green field (inheriting Artists' Rifles traditions); all are current issue; Ef/R.
208 Lance-corporal; **209** Corporal; **210** Sergeant; **211–12** Staff sergeant; **213** Warrant
Officer class 2; **214** Regimental quarter-master sergeant; **215** Warrant Officer class 1.

214

215

EPAULETTE SLIDES

216

217

218

216. Belgian 1st Para Battalion of Regiment Para-Commado, current; yellow metal for officers and recruits, white for NCOs; M/C. (The beret badge follows a similar pattern, but is larger.)

217. Oman, Sultan's Special Forces (Major), working dress, current; black and white crown on purple, background green cotton; Ef/R.

218. Oman, Sultan's Special Forces (Major), shirt, current; gold metal on green cotton; M/R.

47

219–Parachute Regiment (non-issue); olive green with black detail; Ec/C. **219** Private; **26.** **220** Lance-corporal; **221** Corporal; **222** Sergeant; **223** Subaltern; **224** Lieutenant; **225** Captain; **226** Major.

224

225

226

227

228

227. Rhodesian Selous Scouts; olive green, black detail; Ec/C.

228. Royal Air Force Regiment; black lettering on olive green field; Ec/C.

229–Royal Marines, Commando qualified (non-issue); olive green with black detail;
36. Ec/C. **229** Marine; **230** Lance-corporal; **231** Corporal; **232** Sergeant; **233** Second Lieutenant; **234** First Lieutenant; **235** Captain; **236** Major.

234   235

236

237   238

237–40. Special Air Service epaulette slides; Ec/C. **237** Lance-corporal; **238** Corporal.

239   240

239 40. Special Air Service; **239** Sergeant; **240** Staff Sergeant.

STABLE BELTS AND BUCKLES

241. Australian North West Mobile Force; gilt buckle, brass fittings, green and orange stripes on grey; MCl/R.

242. Australian 1 Commando Regiment; black buckle with badge, green and black cloth, white metal fitting; MC/R.

243. Special Air Service Regiment, first pattern Victor Buckle; white metal buckle and fitting, blue cloth; MC/C.

244. Special Air Service Regiment, second pattern; white metal buckle and fittings, blue cloth; MC/C.

245. Parachute Regiment, first pattern Victor buckle; white metal buckle and fittings, maroon cloth; MC/C.

246. Parachute Regiment, second pattern; white metal buckle and fittings, maroon cloth; MC/C.

247. Rhodesian SAS; blue cloth, metal buckle and fittings; Cl-M/R.

248. Rhodesian Selous Scouts; green cloth, white metal buckle and fittings; Cl-M/R.

249. 21 Special Air Service Regiment plate from officer's cartridge belt; brass; B/C.

54

UNOFFICIAL UNIT EMBLEMS

250

251

252

253

250. Parachute EOD (Explosives Ordnance Disposal) Section 421, EOD Company, Royal Army Ordnance Corps (recently changed back to Special Forces EOD Section); grey field, red and yellow flames, black detail; P/R.

251. Parachute EOD Section 421; RAOC; grey field, white parachute, light blue wings, black lettering black and orange grenade, red flames, overlocked in grey; Ec/R.

252. Royal Marines Mountain and Arctic Warfare Cadre; light blue inner field, dark blue outer field, orange lettering, circlets and divide, red dagger, black ice-pick and ski poles, green and white mountain, white snowflake; Sw/R.

253. Royal Marines Special Boat Squadron; dark blue field, white paddles and lettering, red wings and parachute, green frog and lily pad; Ef/R.

REGIMENT AND UNIT ASSOCIATION INSIGNIA

254 255 256

257

258

259

260

262 261 263

254. Airborne Brotherhood (Airborne Forces Security Fund).

255. Airborne Forces.

256. Commando.

257. French SAS (Amicale des Ancien Parachutistes SAS & Commandos de France Libre).

258. GQ parachute award.

259. Irvin parachute award.

260. Parachute Regiment Association.

261. Parachute Regiment Association blazer button.

262. Parachute Regiment Association cufflink.

263. Royal Marines Association.

264. Royal Marine Commando Association, The Green Beret; royal blue field, black overlock and triangle, red dagger and lettering, green beret and yellow badge; Ec/R.

265. The Green Beret Association.

266. Special Air Service Regiment.

267. Special Air Service Regiment Association;

268. blazer badge;

269. cuff badge;

270. cufflink.

271. Special Forces Club;

272. cufflink. (The logo represents the letters 'SOE' in Morse code.)

REGIMENT, UNIT AND ASSOCIATION TIES

273. Oman, Sultan's Special Forces; blue field, Omani SSF wings, purple diagonal; Sw/R.

274. Oman, British Army Training Team (SAS 1970–5); dark blue field, white bat and Sultan's arms; Sw/R.

275. Special Forces Club; dark blue field, yellow parachute with white Morse logo; Sw/R.

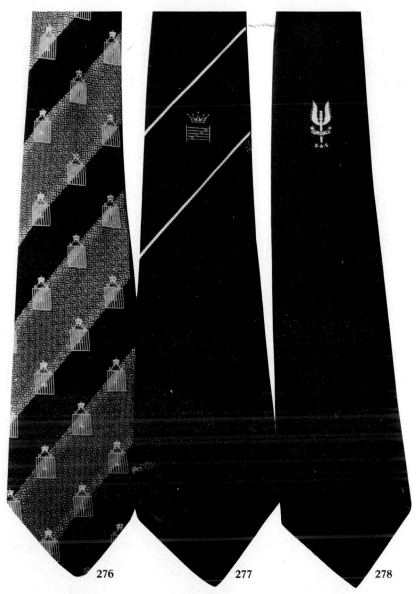

276. Operation 'Nimrod' (official); diagonal dark blue and grey stripes with white devices; Sw/R.

277. Operation 'Nimrod' (unofficial SAS and Diplomatic Protection Group of the Metropolitan Police, London); dark blue field, maroon and light blue diagonals, yellow gate and crown; Ec/R.

278. Special Air Service Regiment; lettering and sword white, dark blue field, wings and scroll light blue, edged in red; P/R.

279. Artists' Rifles and 21 SAS; grey field, black diagonals; Sw/C.

280. Special Air Service Regiment; dark blue field, scroll & wings light blue, sword white; Sw/C.

281. Commando; dagger (various colours) green field; Sw/C.

282. Combined Operations and Joint Services Amphibious Warfare School; red detail, blue field; Sw/C.

283. Royal Marines Special Boat Squadron; red canoe, diver and para wings, blue field; P/R.

284. The Green Beret (Commando Association); green beret, white dagger, red pommel, white scroll, blue field; P/R.

61

285   286

285. Parachute Regiment and Airborne Forces Association; white parachute regiment badge and laurels, blue Pegasus, maroon field; Ec/C.

286. Parachute Regiment; white parachute, light blue wings, maroon field; Sw/C.

REGIMENT, UNIT AND ASSOCIATION PLAQUES

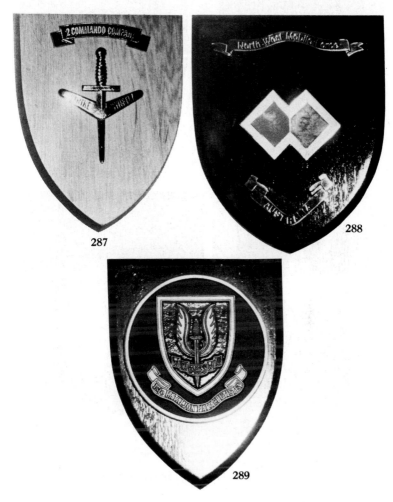

287

288

289

287. Australian 1 Commando Regiment (2 Company, Melbourne); green scroll, white dagger, gold boomerang.

288. Australian North West Mobile Force; green and orange diamonds with pink border.

289. Belgian Bataljon Parachutisen, Regiment Para-Commando; dark blue field, red shield and gold detail.

290. Belgian Battalion, Regiment Para-Commando; black field, red dagger, gold lettering.

291. Belgian Centre Entrainement Commando, Regiment Para-Commando; red detail, dark blue field, gold lettering.

292. Parachute Regiment; red field, light blue stripes and silver badge.

293. Royal Air Force Regiment 2 Field (Parachute) Squadron; light blue circlet, white field, gold detail.

294

295

296

294. 148 (Meiktila) Commando Forward Observation Battery, Royal Artillery Naval Gunfire Support; red detail, blue circle, white parachute, light blue wings, dark blue field.

295. Royal Marines Commando Training Centre; gold detail and scroll, red and green stripe field, black lettering.

296. Royal Marines Mountain and Arctic Warfare Cadre; two quarters silver field, two quarters dark blue field, white parachute, dark blue wings, red dagger, white snowflake green, white and black mountain device, red MAWC tactical sign.

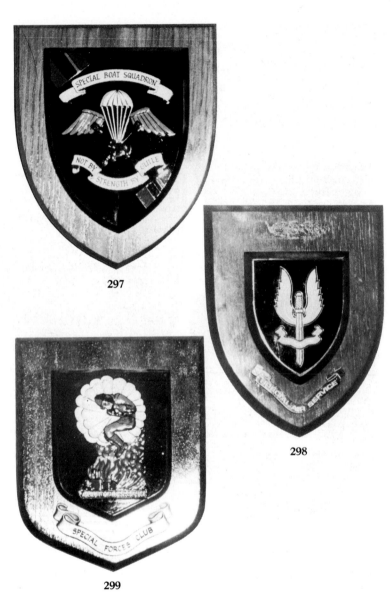

297

298

299

297. Royal Marines Special Boat Squadron.

298. Special Air Service Regiment; dark blue field, silver sword, blue wings and scroll edged in red.

299. Special Forces Club; dark blue field, white parachute, brown figure, red, orange, yellow buildings and flames, grey panel.

INDEX

Bronze badge of the Greek Sacred Squadron, part of 'L' Detachment SAS Brigade and 1 SAS during World War Two. The motto is an ancient Spartan exhortation to 'carry your shield or be carried on it'. Originally a Greek cap badge, this was worn by the Squadron on the battle dress breast pocket; BM/U.